CW00498818

Mini Knit Dolls
Book 5

Little People At Work

EMBER LIM

Copyright © 2012 Ember Lim

All rights reserved. No part of this publication may be reproduced, stored in a retrieval system, or transmitted, in any form or by any means, electronic, mechanical, photocopying, recording, or otherwise without the prior permission of the copyright holder.

ISBN-10: 1481086790
ISBN-13: 978-1481086790

CONTENTS

GENERAL INSTRUCTIONS

Measurement

The basic dolls are about 7.5 cm (3 inches) tall. I use 4-ply 100% acrylic yarn and 2 pairs of 2.25 mm (UK size 13, US size 1) knitting needles. You can change the yarn and needle size to get a bigger or smaller doll.

Basic Materials Required

4-Ply Yarn	as listed
Knitting Needles	2 pairs, 2.25 mm (UK size 13, US size 1)
	1 pair, 4 mm (UK size 8, US size 6)
Yarn Needle	1
Sewing Needle	1
Sewing Thread	black
Embroidery Thread	reddish color for mouth
Powder Blush	reddish for cheek
Cotton Buds	to apply powder blush
Black Round Beads	2 per doll, 2 mm, black
Soft Thick Yarn	for doll's hair
Fiberfill	

Note: Use 2.25 mm knitting needles unless otherwise directed.

Safety

A little common sense should be used when it comes to safety in toys. If the finished toys are to be handled by a small child, you should substitute felt for eyes or embroider them with yarn. If wire has been used in the original instructions, you should either leave it out, or substitute with embroidery where possible.

Yarn – Main Body, Arms and Legs

These instructions work well whether you are using 2-ply, 4-ply, 8-ply or double knitting yarn (with the appropriate size knitting needles) to make the basic doll. You can use any make of yarn, although I find the 2-ply baby yarns too soft. I personally prefer 100% acrylic yarns as these are stiffer and they hold the shape better.

Yarn – Hair

For the hair, you should get very soft yarn. I have used Patons' Zhivago for the shiny effect and Cleckheaton's Folklore and Cleckheaton's Nurture for the tinted hair look. Getting the color right is also important. When you find the color you like, buy a couple of balls and that should last you for a very long time. If you are making fashion dolls, don't be afraid to try colors such as blue, pink and purple.

Yarn – Miscellaneous

For beards, eyebrows and sheep's wool, use furry or eyelash yarns. Where the items are required to look softer for example, a cloak, I use either a 2 or 3-ply yarn.

Tension

Surprisingly, tension is not important for these dolls. Working with different tensions tends to give each doll a different character.

Stuffing

For best results use Fiberfil and stuff the head lightly. This will allow you to twist the head when necessary.

Shape the neck by winding matching yarn round the first row of the head and tie tightly. You get the most mobility with the head if you can stuff the head a little past the neck portion, tie tightly for the neck and then stuff the rest of the body.

Accessories

As you make the dolls, keep an eye out for odd shaped beads and sequins as well as discarded materials with which you can make accessories for the dolls. For example, the crown for one of the wise men in Book 4 is cut out from the collated plastic that holds the nails of a nail gun.

Miscellaneous

Check out www.collectibledoll.co for beginner's instructions, tips and tricks of assembling the dolls, a range of single patterns, assorted little balls of yarn, travel-size bamboo knitting needles and suggestions on how to use your knitted dolls.

ASSEMBLING AND FINISHING UP

The following instructions are common for all the dolls unless otherwise stated:

ASSEMBLING
The Body Of The Doll

Join the row ends from the head downwards to the top of the legs (X on Diagram A) so that the right side of the work is showing outwards.

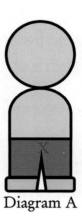

Diagram A

Stuff the body with fiberfill lightly. Do not overstuff unless you want a fat doll. Sew the front of the body to the back of the body at point X.

Join the row ends of each leg together so as to form 2 legs. Stuff a little fiberfill in each leg if necessary. Stuffing for the leg is not necessary if your finished doll is about 7.5 cm (3 inches) or less.

Sew the soles of the shoes together at the base using matching yarn. Fasten off. (Refer to Pg 12 for more details.)

Head And Face

Shape the neck by winding matching yarn round the first row of the head and tie tightly.

Diagram B

Using red embroidery thread, sew a V stitch in the centre lower half of the face. This is the doll's mouth. (Refer Diagram B)

Using the diagram as a guide, sew one eye at a time, pulling the bead so that it is embedded inside the face. Anchor the first eye by ending with a back stitch at the back of the head. Sew the second eye in the same way.

Hair Fringe
Where the doll has a fringe, make 2 or 3 small loops with hair color and sew them at the front of the head. (Refer Diagram B)

SHAPING DOLL'S SHOES AND SANDALS
Sew the soles by stitching at the two red arrows and pulling the sides together as shown in Diagram C. Wind yarn around each foot as shown in Diagram D and Diagram E to complete the sandals.

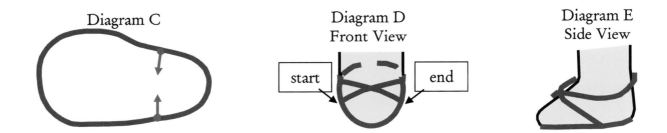

Diagram C

Diagram D
Front View

start   end

Diagram E
Side View

ATTACHING GARMENT PIECE TO DOLL
Different colored yarns are used in the diagram below to show the steps clearly. Use matching yarn to join when you are sewing.

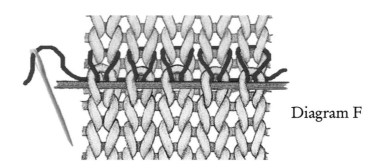

Diagram F

When you have finished, pull out the yarn threaded through the top row of the garment piece – represented by the red yarn in the Diagram F.

FINISHING UP
Belt
Wind yarn, about 2 or 3 times, around the waist of the doll to make the belt. Tie with a dead knot in front of the doll.

Arms
Sew the arms on both sides of the body, positioning them as seen in the photo.

Headband
Wind yarn, about 2 or 3 times, around the head of the doll, on top of the headgear if there is one. Tie with a dead knot on one side of the head.

Cheeks
Using the cotton bud, apply a little blush on both cheeks. If the doll has beard, apply the blush before sewing the beard.

Accessories
Most of the accessories used by the dolls can be sewn on. Failing that, glue the items on and allow to dry thoroughly.

Stitches

Blanket Stitch   Feather Stitch   Diagonal Stitch

1 CHEF

MATERIALS REQUIRED

Basic Materials on Page 3
Flat Gold Button for tray
Blue Tack
Acrylic Paint
Beads – red for cherries
Beads – black for buttons
Drinking Straw
Toothpick
Glue

Item	Yarn Color
Body	Skin Color
Shoes	Black
Hat Uniform	White
Hair	Brown/Black

Knitting Instructions

Legs (make 2)

Row 1:	Leave a long tail at the beginning for shaping shoes. Cast on 20 stitches with shoes color.
Row 2:	Knit to end of row.
Row 3:	Knit 2 stitches together to end of row. Leave enough yarn to tie and break off. (10 stitches)
Row 4:	Change to uniform color; knit to end of row.
Row 5:	Purl to end of row.
Row 6:	Knit to end of row.
Row 7–8:	Repeat Row 5 and 6 alternately. Leave enough yarn to tie and break off.

Leave the stitches of Leg 1 on the knitting needle. Use the second set of knitting needles to begin Leg 2.

Leg 2, Body And Head (Continue from Row 8 of Leg 2)

Row 9:	Continue with uniform color; purl to end of row. Join to Leg 1 and continue to purl to the end of the row. (20 stitches)
Row 10:	Knit to end of row.
Row 11–12:	Knit to end of row.
Row 13:	Purl to end of row.
Row 14–15:	Repeat Row 12 and 13 alternately. Leave enough yarn to tie and break off.
Row 16:	Change to skin color; knit to end of row.
Row 17:	Purl to end of row.
Row 18:	Knit to end of row.
Row 19–27:	Repeat Row 17 and 18 alternately, ending with purl.
Row 28:	Knit 2 stitches together to end of row. Leave enough yarn to sew row ends together and break off. (10 stitches)

Thread through the stitches on the knitting needle. Fasten off tightly.

Arms (make 2)

Row 1:	Cast on 4 stitches with skin color.
Row 2:	Knit twice into every stitch to end of row. Leave enough yarn to tie and break off. (8 stitches)
Row 3:	Change to uniform color; knit to end of row.
Row 4:	Knit to end of row.
Row 5:	Purl to end of row.
Row 6–10:	Repeat Row 4 and 5 alternately, ending with knit.
Row 11:	Purl 2 stitches together to end of row. Leave enough yarn to sew the row ends together and break off. (4 stitches)

Thread through the stitches on the knitting needle. Fasten off tightly. Join the row ends together.

Toque Blanche (Chef's Hat) (make 1)

Row 1:	Cast on 24 stitches with hat color.
Row 2–13:	Knit to end of row.
Row 14:	Knit twice into every stitch to end of row. (48 stitches)
Row 15:	Purl to end of row.
Row 16:	Repeat Row 14. (96 stitches)
Row 17:	Purl to end of row.
Row 18:	Knit 2 together to end. (48 stitches)
Row 19:	Purl to end of row.
Row 20–23:	Repeat Row 18 and 19 alternately, ending with purl. (12 stitches on Row 23.)

Thread through the stitches on the knitting needle. Pull tightly and fasten off. Join the row ends together.

Assembling The Body Of The Doll
Assemble the doll's body, shape the shoes and sew on a fringe as shown on Page 5 and 6.

FINISHING UP
Finish up the dolls as instructed on Page 7 for Arms and Cheeks.

Shirt Hem And Buttons (Refer to photo of doll)
Starting at the back of the doll, sew blanket stitches with matching thread at the bottom edge of the shirt and diagonally across the chest. Sew black beads on the diagonal blanket stitches.

Toque Blanche
Sew on the Toque Blanche so that the fringe is just showing in front.

Tray
Sew the button onto one of the hands so that the flat surface is facing upwards.

Cupcakes
Cut a short length of plastic drinking straw, about 0.5cm (about ¼ inch). This will form the side of the cupcake. Push some Blue Tack into the straw and shape the top of the cupcake. Paint with acrylic paint. While the paint is wet, put a red bead on top as cherry. Make as many as will fit on the tray. Decorate cupcake toppings as you wish.

Rolling Pin
Cut a short length of drinking straw, about 1.5cm (about ¾ inch). Put a toothpick through the center of the straw and hold in place with some Blue Tack. Paint with acrylic paint.

Cut off one of the sharp ends of the toothpick but leave the other sharp end so that you can poke it through the hand. Apply glue to hold the stick in place.

2 MAGICIAN

MATERIALS REQUIRED

Basic Materials on Page 3
Toothpick

Item	Yarn Color
Body	Skin Color
Shoes Shirt Gloves Belt Rabbit	White
Tuxedo Hat	Black
Hair	Brown

Knitting Instructions

Legs (make 2)

Row 1:	Leave a long tail at the beginning for shaping shoes. Cast on 20 stitches with shoe color.
Row 2:	Knit to end of row.
Row 3:	Knit 2 stitches together to end of row. Leave enough yarn to tie and break off. (10 stitches)
Row 4:	Change to trousers color; knit to end of row.
Row 5–6:	Knit to end of row.
Row 7:	Purl to end of row.
Row 8:	Knit to end of row. Leave enough yarn to tie and break off. (10 stitches).

Leave the stitches of Leg 1 on the knitting needle. Use the second set of knitting needles to begin Leg 2.

Leg 2, Body And Head (Continue from Row 8 of Leg 2)

Row 9:	Continue with trousers color; purl to end of row. Join to Leg 1 and continue to purl to the end of the row. Leave enough yarn to tie and break off. (20 stitches)
Row 10:	Knit to end of row.
Row 11:	Purl to end of row.
Row 12:	Knit 9 stitches in trousers color, 2 stitches in shirt color, 9 stitches in trousers color.
Row 13:	Purl 9 stitches in trousers color, 2 stitches in shirt color, 9 stitches in trousers color.
Row 14–15:	Repeat Row 12 and 13.
Row 16:	Change to skin color; knit to end of row.
Row 17:	Purl to end of row.
Row 18:	Knit to end of row.
Row 19–27:	Repeat Row 17 and 18 alternately, ending with purl.

Row 28:	Knit 2 stitches together to end of row. Leave enough yarn to sew row ends together and break off. (10 stitches)

Thread through the stitches on the knitting needle. Fasten off tightly.

Arms (make 2)

Row 1:	Cast on 4 stitches with gloves color.
Row 2:	Knit twice into every stitch to end of row. (8 stitches)
Row 3:	Purl to end of row. Leave enough yarn to tie and break off.
Row 4:	Change to tuxedo color; knit to end of row.
Row 5:	Purl to end of row.
Row 6:	Knit to end of row.
Row 7–10:	Repeat Row 5 and 6 alternately, ending with knit.
Row 11:	Purl 2 stitches together to end of row. Leave enough yarn to sew the row ends together and break off. (4 stitches)

Thread through the stitches on the knitting needle. Fasten off tightly. Join the row ends together.

Tuxedo Tails (make 2)

Row 1:	Cast on 1 stitch with tuxedo color.
Row 2:	Knit twice into every stitch. (2 stitches)
Row 3:	Purl to end of row.
Row 4:	Knit twice into the every stitch to end of row. (4 stitches)
Row 5:	Purl to end of row. Leave enough yarn to tie and break off.

Leave the stitches of Tuxedo Tail 1 on the knitting needle. Use the second set of knitting needles to begin Tuxedo Tail 2.

Join The 2 Tuxedo Tails Together (Continue from Row 5 of Tuxedo Tail 2.)

Row 6:   Continue in tuxedo color; knit to end of row. Join to Coat Tail 1 and continue to knit to the end of the row. (8 stitches)

Row 7:   Purl to end of row. Leave enough yarn to sew coat tails to coat and break off.

Using a different colored yarn, thread through the stitches on the knitting needle and break off. Leave the piece until ready for assembly.

Rabbit Body (make 1)

Row 1:   Leave long yarn at the beginning to make rabbit's tail. Cast on 12 stitches with rabbit color.

Row 2:   Knit to end of row.

Row 3:   Purl to end of row.

Row 4-13:   Repeat Row 2 and 3 alternately ending with purl. Leave enough yarn to tie and break off.

Set aside until ready for assembly.

Rabbit Ears (make 2)

Row 1:   Cast on 4 stitches with rabbit color.

Row 2:   Knit to end of row.

Row 3:   Knit 1, purl 2, knit 1.

Row 4–5 :   Repeat Row 2 and 3.

Row 6:   Knit 2 together to end of row. (2 stitches)

Row 7:   Knit 2 together. (1 stitch). This forms the tip of the ear.

Cut yarn and cast off by pulling the cut yarn through the last loop and pull tightly. Break off yarn.

Making Up The Rabbit (Diagram 2.1.)
Stuff the body lightly with fiberfill. To shape the neck, use 2 strands of sewing threads and tie tightly, making the head slightly bigger than the body.

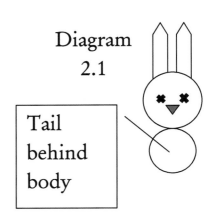

Diagram 2.1

Tail behind body

Using red embroidery thread, sew the nose, making a little triangle as shown in Diagram 2.1. Using black embroidery thread, sew the eyes as shown in the diagram.

Sew the ears to the top of the head. Pull all excess white yarn through the lower body and out to where the tail would be. Cut yarn, leaving enough to make the tail. Unravel yarn and trim into a short bob tail.

Hat A (Make 1)

Row 1:	Cast on 21 stitches with hat color.
Row 2:	Knit to end of row.
Row 3:	Purl to end of row.
Row 4–5:	Repeat Rows 2 and 3.
Row 6:	(Knit 1, knit twice into the next stitch) to end, knit 1. (31 stitches)
Row 7:	Purl to end of row.
Row 8:	Cast off.

Break off, leaving enough yarn to sew the row ends and the cast-off edges to Hat C. Leave aside until ready for assembly.

Hat B (Make 1)

Row 1:   Cast on 21 stitches with hat color.
Row 2:   Knit twice into every stitch to end of row. (42 stitches)
Row 3:   Cast off.

Leave aside Hat B until ready for assembly.

Hat C (Make 1)

Row 1:   Cast on 40 stitches with hat color.
Row 2:   Knit to end of row.
Row 3:   Cast off.

Diagram 2.2

Break off, leaving enough yarn for sewing. Starting at one end, roll up the piece firmly. so that you have a round base for the crown of the hat. Pin and sew the row ends in place. (Diagram 2.2)

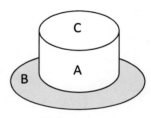

Diagram 2.3

Making Up The Hat (Diagram 2.3)

Wrap Hat A piece around the rolled up piece of Hat C, matching the top ends together. Sew the inner brim of Hat B onto Hat A.

Assembling The Body Of The Doll

Assemble the doll's body, shape the shoes and sew on a fringe as shown on Page 5 and 6.

FINISHING UP

Finish up the dolls as instructed on Page 7 for Arms and Cheeks.

Tuxedo Tails

Attach the tuxedo tails to the back of the doll's body as shown in Attaching Garment Piece to Doll on Page 7.

Hat
Sew the hat onto the head of the doll.

Rabbit
Sew the rabbit onto one of the hands.

Magician's Wand
Cut off one sharp end of a tooth pick. Paint the toothpick black, leaving the blunt tip which is painted silver. Stick the sharp end of the toothpick into the other hand and then cut off the sharp end, leaving a short extended blunt end of the tooth pick coming out from the hand. (Refer to photo of doll)

3 FISHERMAN

MATERIALS REQUIRED

Basic Materials on Page 3
Silver Netting

Item	Yarn Color
Body	Skin Color
Boots	Black
Fishing Waders Hat Belt	Yellow
Shirt	Blue
Hair Color	Brown/Black

Knitting Instructions

Legs (make 2)

Row 1:	Leave a long tail at the beginning for shaping boots. Cast on 20 stitches with boots yarn.
Row 2:	Knit to end of row.
Row 3:	Knit 2 stitches together to end of row. (10 stitches)
Row 4–5:	Knit to end of row. Leave enough yarn to tie and break off.
Row 6:	Change to fishing waders color; knit to end of row.
Row 7:	Purl to end of row.
Row 8:	Knit to end of row. Leave enough yarn to tie and break off. (10 stitches)

Leave the stitches of Leg 1 on the knitting needle. Use the second set of knitting needles to begin Leg 2.

Leg 2, Body And Head (Continue from Row 8 of Leg 2)

Row 9:	Continue with fishing waders color; purl to end of row. Join to Leg 1 and continue to purl to the end of the row. (20 stitches)
Row 10:	Knit to end of row. Leave enough yarn to tie and break off.
Row 11:	Purl 7 stitches in shirt color, 6 stitches in fishing waders color, 7 stitches in shirt color.
Row 12:	Knit 7 stitches in shirt color, 6 stitches in fishing waders color, 7 stitches in shirt color.
Row 13:	Repeat Row 11. Leave enough yarn to tie and break off.
Row 14:	Continue in shirt color; knit to end of row.
Row 15:	Purl to end of row.
Row 16:	Change to skin color; knit to end of row.
Row 17:	Purl to end of row.
Row 18:	Knit to end of row.

| Row 19–27: | Repeat Row 17 and 18 alternately, ending with purl. |
| Row 28: | Knit 2 stitches together to end of row. Leave enough yarn to sew row ends together and break off. (10 stitches) |

Thread through the stitches on the knitting needle. Fasten off tightly.

Arms (make 2)

Row 1:	Cast on 4 stitches with skin color.
Row 2:	Knit twice into every stitch to end of row. (8 stitches)
Row 3:	Purl to end of row. Leave enough yarn to tie and break off.
Row 4:	Change to shirt color; knit to end of row.
Row 5 –6:	Knit to end of row.
Row 7:	Purl to end of row.
Row 8–10:	Repeat Row 6 and 7 alternately, ending with knit.
Row 11:	Purl 2 stitches together to end of row. Leave enough yarn to sew the row ends together and break off. (4 stitches)

Thread through the stitches on the knitting needle. Fasten off tightly. Join the row ends together.

Fisherman's Hat (make 1)

Row 1:	Cast on 30 stitches with hat color.
Row 2–5:	Knit to end of row.
Row 6	Cast off 4 stitches; knit to end of row. (26 stitches)
Row 7:	Cast off 4 stitches; knit 9 stitches, knit 2 stitches together, knit 10 stitches. (21 stitches)
Row 8:	Knit to end of row.
Row 9:	Purl to end of row.
Row 10:	Knit 8 stitches, knit 2 stitches together, knit 1 stitch, knit 2 stitches together, knit 8 stitches. (19 stitches)

Row 11:   Purl to end of row.
Row 12:   Knit 6 stitches, knit 2 stitches together, knit 3 stitches, knit 2 stitches together, knit 6 stitches. (17 stitches)
Row 13:   Purl to end of row.
Row 14:   Knit 6 stitches, knit 2 stitches together, knit 1 stitch, knit 2 stitches together, knit 6 stitches. (15 stitches)
Row 15:   Purl to end of row.

Thread through the stitches on the knitting needle. Fasten off tightly. Join the row ends together, including the cast off edges which forms the back of the hat.

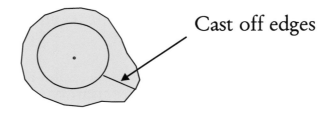

Cast off edges

Assembling The Body Of The Doll
Assemble the doll's body, shape the shoes and sew on a fringe as shown on Page 5 and 6.

FINISHING UP
Finish up the doll as instructed on Page 7 for Belt, Arms and Cheeks.

Hat
Sew the hat onto the head with matching yarn. Add a strap for the hat with matching yarn.

Net
Cut a piece of silver netting about 7.5 cm by 7.5 cm (3 inches by 3 inches). Sew the netting onto the hands and spread out the net as shown in the photograph.

4 MILKMAID

MATERIALS REQUIRED

Basic Materials on Page 3
Silver cord

Item	Yarn Color
Body	Skin Color
Dress	Blue
Apron Sleeves Milk	White
Shoes	Brown
Bucket	Tan
Hair	Yellow

Knitting Instructions

Legs (make 2)

Row 1:	Leave a long tail at the beginning for shaping shoes. Cast on 20 stitches with shoes color.
Row 2:	Knit to end of row.
Row 3:	Knit 2 stitches together to end of row. Leave enough yarn to tie and break off. (10 stitches)
Row 4:	Change to skin color; knit to end of row.
Row 5:	Purl to end of row.
Row 6:	Knit to end of row.
Row 7–8:	Repeat Row 5 and 6 alternately, ending with knit. (10 stitches) Leave enough yarn to tie and break off.

Leave the stitches of Leg 1 on the knitting needle. Use the second set of knitting needles to begin Leg 2.

Leg 2, Body And Head (Continue from Row 8 of Leg 2)

Row 9:	Continue with skin color; purl to end of row. Join to Leg 1 and continue to purl to the end of the row. Leave enough yarn to tie and break off. (20 stitches)
Row 10:	Change to dress color; knit to end of row.
Row 11:	Purl to end of row. Leave enough yarn to tie and break off.
Row 12:	Knit 7 stitches in dress color, 6 stitches in apron color, 7 stitches in dress color.
Row 13:	Purl 7 stitches in dress color, 6 stitches in apron color, 7 stitches in dress color.
Row 14:	Change to dress color; knit to end of row.
Row 15:	Purl to end of row. Leave enough yarn to tie and break off.
Row 16:	Change to skin color; knit to end of row.
Row 17:	Purl to end of row.

Row 18:	Knit to end of row.
Row 19–27:	Repeat Row 17 and 18 alternately, ending with purl.
Row 28:	Knit 2 stitches together to end of row. Leave enough yarn to sew row ends together and break off. (10 stitches)

Thread through the stitches on the knitting needle. Fasten off tightly.

Arms (make 2)

Row 1:	Cast on 4 stitches with skin color.
Row 2:	Knit twice into every stitch to end of row. (8 stitches)
Row 3:	Purl to end of row. Leave enough yarn to tie and break off.
Row 4:	Change to sleeves color; knit to end of row.
Row 5:	Purl twice into every stitch to end of row. (16 stitches)
Row 6:	Knit to end of row.
Row 7:	Purl to end of row.
Row 8:	Repeat Row 6.
Row 9:	Purl 2 stitches together to end of row. (8 stitches)
Row 10:	Knit 2 stitches together to end of row. Leave enough yarn to sew the row ends together and break off. (4 stitches)

Thread through the stitches on the knitting needle. Fasten off tightly. Join the row ends together. Wind sleeves color yarn round the hand at the base of the sleeves to make the sleeve cuff.

Skirt (make 1)

Row 1:	Cast on 30 stitches with dress color.
Row 2:	Knit 1 stitch, wind yarn clockwise under and then over the right needle, knit 2 stitches together) to end of row. (30 stitches)
Row 3:	Knit to end of row.

Row 4:	Purl to end of row.
Row 5–6:	Repeat Row 3 and 4 alternately, ending with purl.
Row 7:	(Knit 1 stitch, knit 2 stitches together) to end of row. Leave enough yarn to sew the row ends together and break off. (20 stitches)

Thread through the stitches on the knitting needle. Fasten off loosely and leave until ready for assembly.

Apron (make 1)

Row 1:	Cast on 12 stitches with apron color.
Row 2:	Knit to end of row.
Row 3:	Purl to end of row.
Row 4–5:	Repeat Row 2 and 3, ending with purl.
Row 6:	Knit 2 stitches together to end of row. Leave enough yarn to attach the apron to the body and break off. (6 stitches)

Thread through the stitches on the knitting needle. Fasten off loosely and leave until ready for assembly.

Milk (make 1)

Row 1:	Cast on 18 stitches with milk color.
Row 2–5:	Knit to end of row.
Row 6:	Cast off. Leave enough yarn to sew the row end and break off.

Diagram 4.1

Starting at one end, roll up the piece firmly. Pin and sew the row ends in place. (Diagram 4.1)

Bucket (make 1)

Row 1:	Cast on 15 stitches with bucket color.

Row 2–3:	Knit to end of row.
Row 4:	(Knit 1 stitch, knit 2 stitches together) to end of row. (10 stitches)
Row 5–7:	Knit to end of row
Row 8:	Cast off. Leave enough yarn to sew the row ends together and break off.

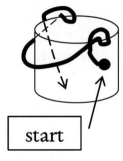

start

Diagram 4.2

Sew row ends together around the roll of milk, matching the bases together. Thread through the stitches on the knitting needle. Fasten off tightly and tuck the ends into the bucket. Using silver cord, make the handle of the pail, hiding the starting and ending stitches inside the bucket as shown in Diagram 4.2.

Assembling The Body Of The Doll
Assemble the doll's body, shape the shoes and sew on a fringe as shown on Page 5 and 6. Use sleeves color instead of skin color for shaping the head so that a collar is formed.

FINISHING UP
Finish up the doll as instructed on Page 7 for Arms and Cheeks.

Bucket
Sew the bucket of milk onto one of the hands so that it sits at the waist and the handle can be seen.

Skirt:
Loop the yarn loosely once more through the stitches to complete the circle. Pull the loop over the doll so that the skirt rest on the waist of the doll. Sew the skirt on to the body with matching yarn.

Apron (Diagram 4.3)
Using the completed apron piece, loop the yarn loosely once more through the stitches to complete the circle. Pull the loop over the doll so that the apron rest on the waist of the doll on top of the skirt. Tie the apron on to the waist ending with a bow at the back.

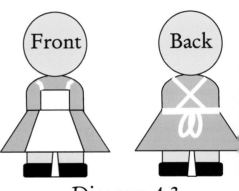
Diagram 4.3

Sew on the apron straps on the shoulders, crossing at the back to hold in place.

Hair
Stick a knitting needle through the head of the doll, so that the needle forms an anchor on both sides of the head, approximately where the ears should be (Diagram 4.4). Using hair color, wind the yarn back and forth on the 2 ends of the needle from the top of the head to the back of the neck.

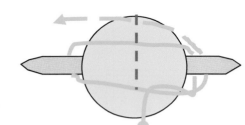
Diagram 4.4
Top View

Using matching needle and threads, stitch on the yarn firmly in the centre of the head, so as to form a centre parting, as indicated by the red dotted line in Diagram 4.4.

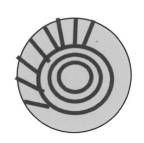
Diagram 4.5
Stitching down
the side hair bun

Stitch the side hair down to hold in place. Remove the knitting needle. Sew back and forth on the yarn so that the hair is shaped like braids on both sides of the head. (Diagram 4.5)

5 FIREMAN

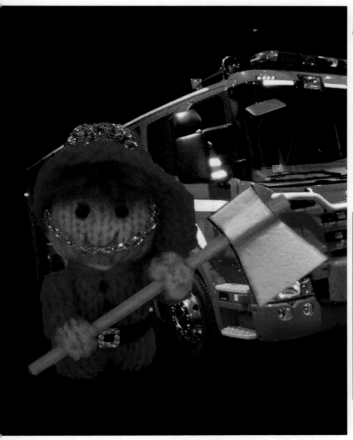

MATERIALS REQUIRED

Basic Materials on Page 3
Toothpick
Cardboard from drink carton
Silver crochet thread
Beads for buttons

Item	Yarn Color
Body	Skin Color
Boots Belt	Black
Uniform Hat	Red
Hair Color	Brown/Black

Knitting Instructions

Legs (make 2)

Row 1:	Leave a long tail at the beginning for shaping boots. Cas on 20 stitches with boots yarn.
Row 2:	Knit to end of row.
Row 3:	Knit 2 stitches together to end of row. (10 stitches)
Row 4–5:	Knit to end of row. Leave enough yarn to tie and break off.
Row 6:	Change to uniform color; knit to end of row.
Row 7:	Purl to end of row.
Row 8:	Knit to end of row. Leave enough yarn to tie and break off. (10 stitches)

Leave the stitches of Leg 1 on the knitting needle. Use the second set o knitting needles to begin Leg 2.

Leg 2, Body And Head (Continue from Row 8 of Leg 2)

Row 9:	Continue with uniform color; purl to end of row. Join to Leg 1 and continue to purl to the end of the row. (20 stitches)
Row 10:	Knit to end of row.
Row 11:	Purl to end of row.
Row 12–15:	Repeat Row 10 and 11 alternately, ending with purl.
Row 16:	Change to skin color; knit to end of row.
Row 17:	Purl to end of row.
Row 18:	Knit to end of row.
Row 19–27:	Repeat Row 17 and 18 alternately, ending with purl.
Row 28:	Knit 2 stitches together to end of row. Leave enough yarn to sew row ends together and break off. (10 stitches)

Thread through the stitches on the knitting needle. Fasten off tightly.

Arms (make 2)

Row 1:	Cast on 4 stitches with skin color.
Row 2:	Knit twice into every stitch to end of row. (8 stitches)
Row 3:	Purl to end of row. Leave enough yarn to tie and break off.
Row 4:	Change to uniform color; knit to end of row.
Row 5–6:	Knit to end of row.
Row 7:	Purl to end of row.
Row 8–10:	Repeat Row 6 and 7 alternately, ending with knit.
Row 11:	Purl 2 stitches together to end of row. Leave enough yarn to sew the row ends together and break off. (4 stitches)

Thread through the stitches on the knitting needle. Fasten off tightly. Join the row ends together.

Fireman's Hat (make 1)

Row 1:	Cast on 30 stitches with hat color.
Row 2–5:	Knit to end of row.
Row 6	Cast off 4 stitches; knit to end of row. (26 stitches)
Row 7:	Cast off 4 stitches; knit 9 stitches, knit 2 stitches together, knit 10 stitches. (21 stitches)
Row 8:	Knit to end of row.
Row 9:	Purl to end of row.
Row 10:	Knit 8 stitches, knit 2 stitches together, knit 1 stitch, knit 2 stitches together, knit 8 stitches. (19 stitches)
Row 11:	Purl to end of row.
Row 12:	Knit 6 stitches, knit 2 stitches together, knit 3 stitches, knit 2 stitches together, knit 6 stitches. (17 stitches)
Row 13:	Purl to end of row.
Row 14:	Knit 6 stitches, knit 2 stitches together, knit 1 stitch, knit 2 stitches together, knit 6 stitches. (15 stitches)

Row 15:   Purl to end of row.

Thread through the stitches on the knitting needle. Fasten off tightly. Join the row ends together, including the cast off edges which form the back of the hat.

Cast off edges

Hat Insignia (make 1)
Row 1:   Cast on 7 stitches with silver crochet thread.
Row 2–4:   Knit to end of row.
Row 5–8:   Cast off 1 stitch at the beginning of each row; knit to end of row. Leave enough yarn to sew the insignia to the hat and break off. (3 stitches)

Sew the insignia to the front of the fireman's hat.

Axe (Diagram 5.1)
Fold the cardboard from a drinks carton into half, with the silver side facing outwards.

Cut out the shape of an axe as shown in Diagram 5.1. The width of the shape when open is about 2.5 cm (1 inch).

Apply glue onto the printed side of the cardboard.

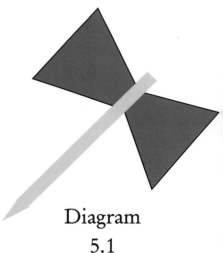

Diagram 5.1

Cut the toothpick so that it is 3 cm (1.5 inch) long. Keep one end pointed.

Press the cardboard down with the toothpick in the centre and allow the glue to dry. The silver side of the cardboard should be facing out.

Assembling The Body Of The Doll
Assemble the doll's body, shape the boots and sew on a fringe as shown on Page 5 and 6.

FINISHING UP
Finish up the doll as instructed on Page 7 for Arms and Cheeks.

Buttons
Sew the beads onto the front of the uniform as buttons.

Belt and Buckle:
Wind black yarn around the waist, tucking in the ends to make it neat. Using silver cord and matching thread, sew the cord onto the front of the belt as shown in Diagram 5.2.

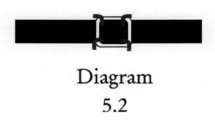

Diagram
5.2

Hat
Sew the hat onto the head with matching yarn. Use the silver crochet thread to make the strap of the hat.

Axe (refer to photo of doll)
Poke the sharp end of the toothpick through the two hands of the fireman as shown in the photograph and apply a little glue. Allow to dry. Cut off the sharp end of the tooth pick leaving a short length showing.

6 FARMER AND WIFE

Farmer & Wife	Yarn Color
Body	Skin Color
Hair Color	Brown
Hat Band	Pink

Farmer	Yarn Color
Shoes Hat Pitchfork Handle	Brown
Dungaree Belt	Blue
Shirt	Pink

Wife	Yarn Color
Sandals Dress	Pink
Carrot Leaves	Green
Basket	Beige
Pinafore Shoulder Frills Hat Sleeve Cuffs	White

MATERIALS REQUIRED

Basic Materials on Page 3
Garden Twist Tie
Acrylic Paint – Orange
Blue Tack
Glue

Knitting Instructions For Farmer

Legs (make 2)

Row 1:	Leave a long tail at the beginning for shaping shoes. Cast on 20 stitches with shoes yarn.
Row 2:	Knit to end of row.
Row 3:	Knit 2 stitches together to end of row. Leave enough yarn to tie and break off. (10 stitches)
Row 4:	Change to dungaree color; knit to end of row.
Row 5–6:	Knit to end of row.
Row 7:	Purl to end of row.
Row 8:	Knit to end of row. Leave enough yarn to tie and break off. (10 stitches)

Leave the stitches of Leg 1 on the knitting needle. Use the second set of knitting needles to begin Leg 2.

Leg 2, Body And Head (Continue from Row 8 of Leg 2)

Row 9:	Continue with dungaree color; purl to end of row. Join to Leg 1 and continue to purl to the end of the row. (20 stitches)
Row 10:	Knit to end of row.
Row 11:	Purl to end of row.
Row 12:	Knit 7 stitches in shirt color, 6 stitches in dungaree color, 7 stitches in shirt color.
Row 13:	Purl 7 stitches in shirt color, 6 stitches in dungaree color, 7 stitches in shirt color. Leave enough yarn to tie and break off.
Row 14:	Change to shirt color; knit to end of row.
Row 15:	Purl to end of row.
Row 16:	Change to skin color; knit to end of row.
Row 17:	Purl to end of row.

Row 18:   Knit to end of row.

Row 19–27:   Repeat Row 17 and 18 alternately, ending with purl.

Row 28:   Knit 2 stitches together to end of row. Leave enough yarn to sew row ends together and break off. (10 stitches)

Thread through the stitches on the knitting needle. Fasten off tightly.

Arms (make 2)

Row 1:   Cast on 4 stitches with skin color.

Row 2:   Knit twice into every stitch to end of row. (8 stitches)

Row 3:   Purl to end of row. Leave enough yarn to tie and break off.

Row 4:   Change to shirt color; knit to end of row.

Row 5–6:   Knit to end of row.

Row 7:   Purl to end of row.

Row 8–10:   Repeat Row 6 and 7 alternately, ending with knit.

Row 11:   Purl 2 stitches together to end of row. Leave enough yarn to sew the row ends together and break off. (4 stitches)

Thread through the stitches on the knitting needle. Fasten off tightly. Join the row ends together.

Farmer's Hat
Hat Brim (make 1)

Row 1:   Cast on 48 stitches with hat color.

Row 2:   Knit to end of row.

Row 3:   Purl to end of row.

Row 4–7:   Repeat Row 2 and 3 alternately, ending with purl.

Row 8:   Knit 2 stitches together; (knit 2 stitches together, cast off) to end of row. Leave enough yarn to sew the row ends together and break off.

Sew the row ends together. Thread the remainder of the thread through the edge of the hat brim to prevent it from curling.

Crown Of Hat (make 1.)

Row 1:   Cast on 26 stitches with hat color.
Row 2:   Knit to end of row.
Row 3:   Purl to end of row.
Row 4–9:   Repeat Rows 2 and 3 alternately, ending with purl.
Row 10:   Knit 2 stitches together to end of row. Leave enough yarn to sew the row ends together and to join the brim to the crown. Break off. (13 stitches)

Using a yarn needle, thread through the stitches on the knitting needle. Pull tightly and fasten off.

Assembling The Hat

Use the remainder of the yarn and join the row ends from the tip of the crown downwards to the base, so that the right side of the work is showing outwards. Join the base of the hat to the inner brim of the hat using matching yarn.

Wind hat band color around the base of the crown and tie a bow. (See photo)

Farmer's Pitchfork (Diagram 6.1)

Bend the Garden Twist Tie into the shape shown in Diagram 6.1. Begin at the dot and end at the arrow.

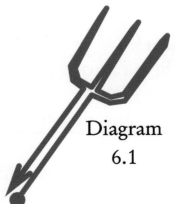

Diagram 6.1

Wind yarn around so that the handle is covered completely.

Put a little glue at the end and hold in place till dry. Bend the tips o the fork so that they are slightly curved.

Assembling The Body Of The Doll
Assemble the doll's body, shape the shoes and sew on a fringe a shown on Page 5 and 6.

FINISHING UP
Finish up the doll as instructed on Page 7 for Arms and Cheeks.

Hat
Sew the hat onto the head with matching yarn.

Dungaree Strap and Belt (Diagram 6.2)
Using dungaree color, make two straps from the dungaree top, going over the shoulders and crossing behind the doll as shown in the diagram.

Use the extra yarn to wind round the waist of the doll to form the belt.

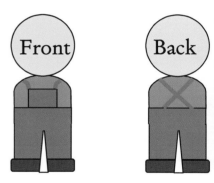

Diagram 6.2

Pitchfork
Sew the pitchfork onto one of the hands.

Knitting Instructions For Farmer's Wife

Legs (make 2)

Row 1:	Leave a long tail at the beginning for shaping sandals Cast on 20 stitches with sandals color. Leave enough yarn to tie and break off.
Row 2:	Change to skin color; knit to end of row.
Row 3:	Purl 2 stitches together to end of row. (10 stitches)

Row 4:	Knit to end of row.
Row 5:	Purl to end of row.
Row 6–8:	Repeat Row 4 and 5 alternately, ending with knit. Leave enough yarn to tie and break off. (10 stitches)

Leave the stitches of Leg 1 on the knitting needle. Use the second set of knitting needles to begin Leg 2.

Leg 2, Body And Head (Continue from Row 8 of Leg 2)

Row 9:	Continue with skin color; purl to end of row. Join to Leg 1 and continue to purl to the end of the row. Leave enough yarn to tie and break off. (20 stitches)
Row 10:	Change to dress color; knit to end of row.
Row 11:	Purl to end of row.
Row 12:	Knit 7 stitches in dress color, 6 stitches in pinafore color, 7 stitches in dress color.
Row 13:	Purl 7 stitches in dress color, 6 stitches in pinafore color, 7 stitches in dress color. Leave enough yarn to tie and break off.
Row 14:	Change to dress color; knit to end of row.
Row 15:	Purl to end of row.
Row 16:	Change to skin color; knit to end of row.
Row 17:	Purl to end of row.
Row 18:	Knit to end of row.
Row 19–27:	Repeat Row 17 and 18 alternately, ending with purl.
Row 28:	Knit 2 stitches together to end of row. Leave enough yarn to sew row ends together and break off. (10 stitches)

Thread through the stitches on the knitting needle. Fasten off tightly.

Arms (make 2)

Row 1:	Cast on 4 stitches with skin color.

Row 2:	Knit twice into every stitch to end of row. (8 stitches)
Row 3:	Purl to end of row.
Row 4:	Knit to end of row.
Row 5:	Purl to end of row. Leave enough yarn to tie and break off.
Row 6:	Change to sleeve cuffs color; knit to end of row.
Row 7:	Knit to end of row. Leave enough yarn to tie and break off.
Row 8:	Change to dress color; knit to end of row.
Row 9:	Purl to end of row.
Row 10:	Knit to end of row.
Row 11:	Purl 2 stitches together to end of row. Leave enough yarn to sew the row ends together and break off. (4 stitches)

Thread through the stitches on the knitting needle. Fasten off tightly. Join the row ends together.

Shoulder Frills (make 2)

Row 1:	Cast on 10 stitches with shoulder frills color.
Row 2:	Cast off the first and last stitch; knit all the other stitches in the row. (8 stitches)
Row 3:	Cast off the first and last stitch; purl all the other stitches in the row. (6 stitches)
Row 4:	Cast off. Leave enough yarn to sew the frills over the shoulders of the doll and break off.

Set aside until ready for assembly.

Skirt (make 1)

Row 1:	Cast on 40 stitches with dress color.
Row 2–4:	Knit to end of row.
Row 5:	Purl to end of row.

Row 6:   Change to pinafore color; knit to end of row.
Row 7:   Purl to end of row.
Row 8:   Knit 2 stitches together to end of row. (20 stitches)
Row 9:   Purl to end of row. Leave enough yarn to sew the row ends together and break off.

Thread through the stitches on the knitting needle. Fasten off loosely and leave until ready for assembly.

Pinafore Frill (make 1)
Row 1:   Cast on 40 stitches with pinafore color.
Row 2:   Knit to end of row.
Row 3:   Cast off.

Leave until ready for assembly.

Wife's Hat
Make the Hat Brim and Crown of Hat as for the Farmer's Hat.

Hat Band (Make 1)
Row 1:   Cast on 26 stitches with hat band color.
Row 2:   Knit 2 stitches, cast off; (knit 1 stitch, cast off) to end of row. Fasten off.

Set aside all hat pieces until doll is ready for assembly.

Basket (Make 1)
Row 1:   Cast on 14 stitches using 2 strands of the basket color.
Row 2:   Knit to end of row. Cut off 1 strand of the yarn and tuck neatly into the basket when assembling. Continue knitting with the remaining strand.

Row 3:   Purl to end of row.

Row 4:   Knit 2 stitches together to end of row. Leave enough yarn to sew the row ends together. (7 stitches)

Using a yarn needle, thread through the stitches on the knitting needle. Pull tightly. Join row ends together and fasten off.

Carrots (Make 3)

Roll Blue Tack into shape of carrot. Apply orange acrylic paint and allow to dry. Cut a short strand of carrot leaves color. Fold yarn into two and push into top of carrot with a little glue. When glue is dry unravel the yarn so that they look like leaves.

Assembling The Body Of The Doll

Assemble the doll's body, shape the sandals and sew on a fringe as shown on Page 5 and 6.

FINISHING UP

Finish up the doll as instructed on Page 7 for Cheeks and Arms. Wind yarn at the base of the sleeves to make the cuffs.

Hat

Assemble the hat as for Farmer's Hat. Sew on the Hat Band at the base of the crown.

Skirt And Pinafore Frill

Loop the yarn loosely once more through the stitches to complete the circle. Pull the loop over the doll so that the skirt rest on the waist of the doll. Sew the skirt on with matching thread. Sew the Pinafore Frill to the bottom edge of the pinafore with matching thread.

Shoulder Frills

Using matching thread, sew each Shoulder Frill to the right and left shoulder of the doll. Begin at the front of the skirt, go over the shoulders and end at the back of the skirt.

Wind pinafore color round the waist of the doll to form the belt.

Basket
Sew the basket onto one of the hands and to part of the pinafore to hold it up.

Carrots
Attach a carrot to one of the hands by sewing the leaves to the hand. Put the rest of the carrots into the basket. Glue in place if desired.

7 SINGER

MATERIALS REQUIRED

Basic Materials on Page 3
Cotton bud
Acrylic paint – red
Old plastic card
Marker pen – black
Metallic red crochet thread
Silver crochet thread

Item	Yarn Color
Body	Skin Color
Shoes Trousers Shirt Sleeves Collar	White
Hair Color	Any Color

Knitting Instructions

Legs (make 2)

Row 1:	Leave a long tail at the beginning for shaping shoes. Cast on 20 stitches with shoe color.
Row 2:	Knit to end of row.
Row 3:	Knit 2 stitches together to end of row. (10 stitches)
Row 4–6:	Knit to end of row.
Row 7:	Purl to end of row.
Row 8:	Knit to end of row. Leave enough yarn to tie and break off. (10 stitches).

Leave the stitches of Leg 1 on the knitting needle. Use the second set of knitting needles to begin Leg 2.

Leg 2, Body And Head (Continue from Row 8 of Leg 2)

Row 9:	Continue with trousers color; purl to end of row. Join to Leg 1 and continue to purl to the end of the row. Leave enough yarn to tie and break off. (20 stitches)
Row 10:	Knit to end of row.
Row 11:	Purl to end of row.
Row 12–15:	Repeat Row 10 and 11 alternately, ending with purl.
Row 16:	Change to skin color; knit to end of row.
Row 17:	Purl to end of row.
Row 18:	Knit to end of row.
Row 19–27:	Repeat Row 17 and 18 alternately, ending with purl.
Row 28:	Knit 2 stitches together to end of row. Leave enough yarn to sew row ends together and break off. (10 stitches)

Thread through the stitches on the knitting needle. Fasten off tightly.

Arms (make 2)

Row 1:	Cast on 4 stitches with skin color.

Row 2:	Knit twice into every stitch to end of row. (8 stitches)
Row 3:	Purl to end of row. Leave enough yarn to tie and break off.
Row 4:	Change to shirt color; knit to end of row.
Row 5:	Purl to end of row.
Row 6:	Knit to end of row.
Row 7–10:	Repeat Row 5 and 6 alternately, ending with knit.
Row 11:	Purl 2 stitches together to end of row. Leave enough yarn to sew the row ends together and break off. (4 stitches)

Thread through the stitches on the knitting needle. Fasten off tightly. Join the row ends together.

Collar (make 1)

Row 1:	Cast on 24 stitches with collar color.
Row 2:	Knit to end of row.
Row 3:	Cast off. Leave enough yarn to sew the collar onto the shirt and break off.

Microphone (Diagram 7.1)

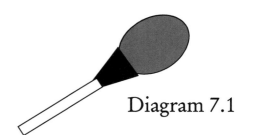

Cut the cotton bud into half, leaving enough of the stick to poke into the hand. Color the base black with marker pen. Paint the top of the microphone red. Leave to dry.

Diagram 7.1

Assembling The Body Of The Doll

Assemble the doll's body and shape the shoes as shown on Page 5 and 6.

FINISHING UP

Finish up the doll as instructed on Page 7 for Arms, Cheeks and Belt.

using the silver crochet thread for the belt. Sew the arms as shown in the photograph or any suitable pose.

Collar
Sew the collar on to the shirt with matching thread.

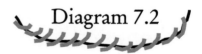

Diagram 7.2

Silver Trimmings on Clothes
Using silver crochet thread, sew trimmings on edge of collar, sleeves and bottom of trousers using a diagonal stitch. (Diagram 7.2)

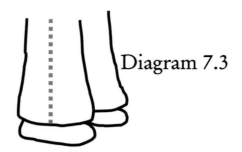

Diagram 7.3

Sew a line of running stitch along the outer side of each trouser leg. (Diagram 7.3)

Hair (Diagram 7.4)
Stitch the yarn at the sewing line with matching thread, indicated by the red dotted line in the diagram.

Pull the yarn down towards the neck, to the length that you want. Hold the yarn in place with a pin and pull the yarn up and stitch at the sewing line.

Head – View From Top
Diagram 7.4

Repeat this until the hair is complete. Remove the pins and stitch the yarn down.

For the lock of hair on the forehead, stick a yarn needle through the head as shown in Diagram 7.4. Wind hair yarn round the needle and then thread through. Pull lightly so as to maintain the curly shape of the lock. Stitch down the base with matching thread.

Guitar (Diagram 7.5)

Make the template for the guitar on paper, cutting and shaping unti
you get the right shape and size. Using the template, cut out 2 piece
using an old plastic card.

Using pins to hold one guitar piece on the doll's body, place one end
of the red metallic crochet thread on the guitar and bring the thread
round the neck of the doll. Cut and glue in place.

Draw an oval shape on the second guitar piece with the marker pen
Glue the two pieces together, sandwiching the thread in the middle.

Diagram 7.5

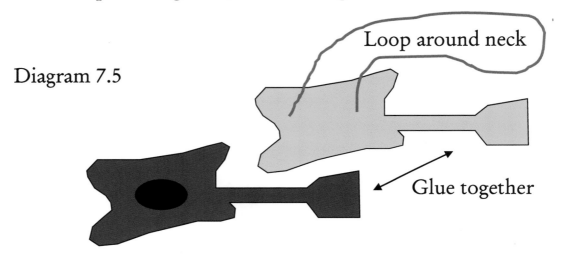

Microphone

Push the stick end of the microphone into the free hand and hold ir
place with glue.

Books by Ember Lim are available online from:

http://www.amazon.com/

To purchase individual patterns visit:
www.collectibledoll.co

(Printed and PDF versions available)

KNITTING BOOKS BY EMBER LIM

Mini dolls to knit and give away or keep as collectibles

MINI
KNIT DOLLS
BOOK 1

Mini Snowmen In
Costumes From
Around The World

MINI
KNIT DOLLS
BOOK 2

Mini Dolls
In Native American
Costumes

MINI
KNIT DOLLS
BOOK 3

Mini Dancing Dolls

MINI KNIT DOLLS
BOOK 4

Mini Nativity Knits
& The Story Of Christmas

MINI KNIT DOLLS
BOOK 5

Little People At Work

WATCH OUT FOR THESE EASY-AND-QUICK-KNITS BY EMBER LIM

Little People At Play

Little Gnomes

Nursery Rhymes Characters

College Friends

Bible Characters

Story Book Characters

Check out www.collectibledoll.co for beginner's instructions, tips and tricks of assembling the dolls, a range of single patterns, assorted little balls of yarn, travel-size bamboo knitting needles and suggestions on how to use your knitted dolls. The Learn To Knit With Ember Lim series is also posted on YouTube.

BOOKS BY EMBER LIM & KEN LOH

ALPHABET A
Blackline Worksheets
And Activities

ALPHABET A
Color Worksheets
And Activities

Everything you need in blackline or color to teach the alphabet A and more in one book – a treasure trove for tired teachers! Thematic activities include games, songs, art projects, food activities, science projects and mathematics.

The books in this series are stand-alone books and can be used in any order. There should be enough material in each book to cover at least two weeks in a classroom or homeschool situation. The handwriting section include practice pages for script as well as cursive fonts.

Permission is granted to make copies of this work provided that such copies are for use in academic classrooms or for personal use - terms and conditions apply.

16220997R00032

Printed in Great Britain
by Amazon